LOYOLA PRESS.

A whole Bunch of Values

Jennifer Moore-Mallinos / Julia Seal

- Altruism, 4
- Attention, 6
- Carefulness, 8
- Charity, 10
- Cleanliness, 12
- Compassion, 14
- Confidence, 16
- Courage, 18
- Curiosity, 20
- Dedication, 22
- Empathy, 24

- Enthusiasm, 26
- Freedom, 28
- Friendship, 30
- Generosity, 32
- Goodness, 34
- Gratitude, 36
- Happiness, 38
- Hard Work, 40
- Honesty, 42
- Humility, 44
- Kindness, 46

Table of

- Love, **48**
- Moderation, **50**
- Motivation, **52**
- Openness, **54**
- Optimism, **56**
- Organization, **58**
- Passion, **60**
- Patience, **62**
- Peace, **64**
- Persistence, **66**
- Respect, **68**
- Responsibility, **70**
- Satisfaction, **72**
- Sensitivity, **74**
- Serenity, **76**
- Sharing, **78**
- Silence, **80**
- Simplicity, **82**
- Sustainability, **84**
- Teamwork, **86**
- Thankfulness, **88**
- Tolerance, **90**
- Trustworthiness, **92**
- Values, Values, Values!, **94**

Contents

Altruism

Every week my brother and I volunteer at the local animal shelter. We donate our time to help take care of the animals. We make sure they have clean, fresh water, we play with them, and we even brush their fur. But most of all we give them lots of hugs and kisses. Spending our time helping the homeless dogs altruistically, **without expecting anything in return,** is not only a kind thing to do; it's also our way to show we care.

Do you do anything altruistically to show that you care for others?

Attention

Whenever Grandma comes to visit, I always make sure she is comfortable. First, I check to see if she is feeling chilly, and then I bring her a blanket and her fuzzy slippers. Grandma likes it when I help make her a cup of tea, too. Grandma says that I'm very attentive and kind. But for me, **making sure Grandma is warm and cozy** is just what I like to do.

Is there somebody you like to pay special attention to?

Carefulness

Everyone knows that you have to look **both ways before crossing the street.** Keeping your eyes and ears open to carefully watch and listen for cars going by helps keep us safe. Holding the hand of a person that you trust, like your dad or older sister, is another way to make sure you stay out of danger. Being careful when you cross the street is a good thing to do!

What are some ways you're careful to keep yourself safe?

Charity

Every year in the holiday season, my school has
a charity drive **to collect cans of food** from all
the families. Our goal is to fill the big bin at the front
of the school with as much food as we can. Once the
bin is full, we take all the food we collected to the
local shelter to help those in need.

Can you think of some other ways that charity helps those in need?

Cleanliness

Do you ever have a hard time keeping your bedroom clean and neat? Me too! Making sure my clothes are in the drawers, my bed is made, and my toys are put away can be a lot of work! But when my bedroom is clean and everything is in its place, **it feels cozier and way more comfortable.**

What do you do to keep your bedroom clean?

Compassion

One night my family went out to eat. After dinner, we took a walk and saw a homeless person holding up a sign asking for help. **I felt sad that he didn't have a home or any food to eat.** I asked my parents if we could buy him food from the restaurant. My mom and dad agreed. The homeless person smiled when I gave him a box with his dinner. Showing that you care about other people is being compassionate.

When was a time that you showed compassion?

Confidence

When my parents brought home my dog, Tucker, I promised that I would look after him. And I do! Mom and Dad are confident that I will take him for a walk every day. I make sure Tucker has clean water and food. I give him lots of love. I know that my parents will always be there for me, too. **Having confidence in yourself and others is a wonderful feeling.**

When was a time you were confident that you could do something new?

Courage

Have you ever done something that scared you, but you did it because it was the right thing to do? Leo always pushed himself to the front of the line, even when my friend was line leader. Being brave and standing up to him is something I did. It took a lot of courage to tell Leo that he should not cut the line. But it worked! And we're best buddies now! **Sometimes doing the right thing can be scary.** So, take a deep breath and try your best.

When was a time that you had to use all your courage to get something done?

Curiosity

The first time I took my puppy, Murph, outside, **he was so excited to explore the world.** So, when he came across a hole in the ground, he was determined to figure out what was down it. While I watched, Murph cautiously poked his head in the hole. Something must have moved because Murph jumped back! Now we were BOTH curious.

All of a sudden a chipmunk came running out of the hole. Murph and I were so surprised!

Do you remember a time when you were super-curious about something new?

Dedication

As a member of my swim team, it is my job to make sure that I go to all the practices and **work as hard as I can all the time.** Everybody on my team is so dedicated that we made a pledge that we would work hard to make it to the championship swim meet. And guess what? Our dedication was worth it because we made it to the championship! Go team!

Is there something that you enjoy dedicating yourself to?

Empathy

Putting yourself in someone else's shoes means that you **try to understand** what they're going through and how they're feeling, especially if you've had the same kind of experience. When my best friend's dog was sick, I knew that she was feeling scared and sad because that was how I felt when my hamster was sick. I got it! Understanding how someone else is feeling shows empathy.

Have you ever put yourself in someone else's shoes?

Enthusiasm

Is there something that you love doing that makes you feel **so happy and full of energy**? Me too! Whenever I visit the amusement park, I'm always excited and eager to go on as many rides as I can. Full of enthusiasm and excitement, I'm even willing to try out the roller coaster that turns upside down! It's so much fun!!! I can't stop smiling!!!

What is something that makes you feel enthusiastic and full of life?

Freedom

Ever since my dad finished putting up the picket fence around our yard, my little sister and our puppy have a new sense of freedom. There is nothing better than **being able to roam freely** in your very own backyard, kicking and chasing a ball around, knowing that it won't roll out onto the street. How fun is that!

Is there a place you like to go that you can run around freely wherever you want?

Friendship

Do you have **a special someone in your life that you really care about**? Me too! Not only am I close friends with Olivia down the street, but my dog, Buster, is my friend, too. Being a friend means that you like spending time together and doing things that you both find fun! Whether it's watching a movie with Olivia or playing fetch with Buster, I enjoy our time together.

What are some things you like to do with your friends?

Generosity

Have you ever given someone you don't even know something they really need? Last year, after hearing about a young family who lost their home in a big storm, we decided to try to help. We gathered food, bottles of water, and clothing and sent it to them. Being as generous as we could to help this family **made everyone feel happy.**

What have you done to be generous to others?

Goodness

Do you have **that special someone who is always there for you,** especially when you are sad? Me too! Whenever I feel a little bit down, my cat seems to know it. To show she loves me and cares about how I feel, she will snuggle up close and purr. Her concern and understanding always seem to help! She is such a good cat!

What do you do to show goodness toward others?

Gratitude

Have you ever been so grateful for something that you couldn't stop saying "thank you"? I will never forget how excited and happy I was when I got a brand-new bicycle on my fourth birthday. I ran to my mom and dad and flew into their arms to show them how much I treasured my present! Being grateful and **showing how much you appreciate something or someone** is a nice thing to do.

When was a time that you showed gratitude?

Happiness

There is nothing I enjoy more on a hot day than a big scoop of ice cream. How can a scoop of coldness bring such happiness and pleasure to a little kid like me? **Ice cream on a hot day is like taking a trip to paradise!** Now that I think about it, I must be my mom and dad's scoop of ice cream because they always tell me that I am their biggest delight!

What brings you happiness?

Hard Work

Is there something that you have to work hard to do? For me it's math! Every night, my mom and I practice my math facts with flash cards. **Sometimes I want to give up,** but Mom keeps telling me that if I practice, practice, practice, doing math will get easier. Mom was right! All my hard work paid off because I got 100% on my last math test!!!

What is something that you have to work hard to do?

Honesty

Sometimes it may be hard to tell the truth,
especially when you know that you made a mistake.
One time I borrowed my sister's pants without asking
and accidently ripped them.

It was only fair for me to be honest and tell her what happened. My sister wasn't happy about her pants, but she was proud of me for being honest.

Did you know that when you are honest with people, they learn to trust you?

Humility

When my brother showed me a different way to tie my shoes, and his way was better, it was hard for me to admit it. But after I accepted that his way was easier and that my laces stayed tied all day, I humbly thanked him for his help. **What would you do if your best friend did something better than you did?** Would you pretend you didn't notice, or would you have the humility to let him know that he did a good job?

What is something that you have learned from a friend?

Kindness

My grandpa has the biggest heart! He's always there for me, especially when I need help putting together a school project. I will never forget all the time we spent building a birdhouse. **Grandpa even gave up watching a football game to help me!** Now I know why we call him a gentle giant. Not only is he big and tall, he's also as gentle and kind.

Who shows you kindness?

Love

Is there someone in your life who makes you feel all warm inside? Thinking about my new baby brother fills me with so much love. He's only a few days old, but I feel like I have known him my whole life. I love holding him and listening to his coos. When his little hand squeezes my finger, I can't help but smile. **How is it possible to be so attached** to such a little guy just a few days old?

Who fills your heart with love?

Moderation

Did you know that if you eat too many sweet
potatoes, your skin can turn orange? And guess
what happens if you do too many sit-ups at
one time? Yep, your muscles will get sore!

Even when we do things that are good for us,
**we need to make sure that we don't go
overboard.** We need to do just enough so that
these things are still good for us. Too much of
a good thing isn't always good! Moderation is key!

What is something you do in moderation?

Motivation

Everybody has something that they are determined to do or be good at. My goal is to be the best gymnast that I can be! I get so excited every week when I go to my gymnastics practice. I practice hard because my motivation is to someday be in the Olympics. The thought of having a gold medal around my neck pushes me to keep trying hard!

What motivates you to work hard?

Openness

Did you know that everybody has their own thoughts and ideas about certain things? Even though we may not agree with other people's ideas, **we should try to listen and understand** what they are saying. It might be as simple as being open to trying something new, like putting chocolate syrup on your toast. You never know, you might like it!

Are you open to trying something new?

Optimism

My teacher, Ms. Mathis, was very optimistic that the whole class would pass the spelling test. Ms. Mathis cheered us on during the test, telling us that we would all be successful because she knew that we had studied hard. And guess what? Having **positive thoughts** about passing the test helped. We all passed! Hooray!

Is there something in your future that you are optimistic about?

Organization

Did you know that putting together a concert isn't that easy unless you're organized? As the conductor of the choir, it's my job to make sure everybody's standing in the right place on stage for the performance. First, we plan where every singer will stand, then we practice getting in line in the right order. That way, when we come out on stage, we don't trip over one another. **Have you ever planned a special event?**

What did you do to make sure it ran smoothly?

Passion

Passion means having **a strong, positive feeling about something that matters to you**, like family. In my house, my mom and dad, my two sisters, and I are all dedicated to making sure that we have family time together.

Every Friday night is family night. No matter what's going on, we all make time to be together, either to play a game, make homemade pizzas, or watch a movie. Family matters!

What is something that you feel passionate about?

Patience

Sometimes I get so mad when I'm in a hurry to learn something new. I remember trying to learn how to use a toy hoop. No matter how much I tried, the hoop kept falling to the ground, and I wanted to give up. But instead, **I slowed down, took a big breath,** and figured out a better way to keep the hoop spinning. Because I was patient and didn't freak out, I did it! I learned that being patient is not always easy when you're in a hurry.

When was the last time you had to show patience?

Peace

Watching all the sleeping puppies snuggled up on top of one another and close to their mama made me smile. They all looked like little angels, resting peacefully without a care in the world. While they dreamed of chasing balls and playing in the grass, **I enjoyed the silence.** I knew that when they all woke up, the quiet, peaceful puppies would come to life.

AHHH, so peaceful.

Persistence

Did you know that putting a puzzle together is not always easy? Some puzzles are so tricky that you just want to give up. But for me, the harder the puzzle, the more persistent I get because **I am determined to figure it out.** Whenever I start a new puzzle, I am so focused on finishing it that I can sit for hours until it's done. My persistence has helped me finish a lot of puzzles!

When has your persistence helped you finish something?

Respect

Is there someone in your life whom you respect? Whenever I think of how much my brother helped when my dad broke his leg, **I feel such admiration for him.** Not only did my brother do all the yard work, but he made sure that the barn animals were cared for, just like Dad would. Keeping up with so many chores was an important job, and my brother stepped up!!!

I really respect my brother!

Responsibility

Being responsible is important, especially when you're in charge of making sure a job gets done. Every week at school our teacher gives us jobs to do. My favorite job is when I'm the "Cleanup Detective." I even get to wear a detective hat! It's my responsibility as detective to inspect the classroom and make sure that everything is put away in the right spot. **My teacher trusts that I'll do a good job** to help keep our classroom neat.

What is something you are responsible for?

Satisfaction

Is there something that you have taken so much pride in doing, that when it was done, **you sat back and smiled?** Me too! At school we had to build a volcano that could erupt! When it was my turn to show my volcano, and it did what it was supposed to do, I felt such satisfaction! I did it!!! I was so satisfied with all my hard work!

I even gave myself a pat on the back for a job well done!

Sensitivity

When somebody is thoughtful and cares about others, they are being sensitive. The other day when my sister, Zaria, and I were riding our bikes in the park, I hit a bump that sent me flying off onto the sidewalk. Before I even knew what happened, Zaria was by my side helping me up.

Seeing that I scraped my knee, Zaria carefully covered my wound with a bandage.

I was touched by how sensitive Zaria was.

Serenity

Being calm and relaxed is a serene feeling.
When my family and I go camping, we always love to
build a campfire, especially at night when everything
is quiet and still. Gazing up at the stars gives me a
sense of serenity and togetherness.

Is there a place you like to go that is quiet
and gives you the feeling of AHHH?

Sharing

Sometimes it's hard to share, especially when it is something you want to keep for yourself. Like last night, I really wanted to eat the last piece of pizza. But since both my dad and I wanted it, we decided to cut it in half. I guess half a slice of pizza is better than none at all! **Sharing is caring!**

How does it make you feel when you share something?

Silence

Have you ever noticed how silent it is when the wind stops blowing and the birds stop singing? Like the wind and the birds, **sometimes we need to be still,** not make any noise, and just listen. Whether it is at school or playing hide-and-seek, being silent is important.

Can you think of other places that are silent? Sshhhh!

Simplicity

My dog's real name is Ruff, but we sometimes call him Easy-Peasy! Ruff likes things to be just that: EASY. So, when I ask Ruff to sit, I keep the instructions short, simple, and to the point. If I make them too complicated and use too many words, he might do something completely different, like roll over. **Sometimes keeping things simple is easier for everyone!**

What are some things that you would like to make simpler?

Sustainability

What is something we can do to keep our Planet Earth healthy? **We can recycle!** Did you know that old tires can be cut into little pieces and put on the playground to keep us safe if we fall? And guess what! Plastic bottles can be made into sweaters, sleeping bags, and even carpeting. How cool is that!

Can you think of other ways we can be sustainable to help protect our planet?

Teamwork

My family likes to work together to get big projects done, like when we painted my bedroom. Even though we had different jobs to do, **we each did what we could to help one another.** I held the ladder for Dad when he was painting the ceiling, and Mom stirred the paint for my brother. It felt good to be part of the painting team. I especially liked my painting hat and overalls!

What are some things you can do to work as a team?

Thankfulness

I am so thankful that I have a loving family.
I appreciate everything that my mom and dad do for me. I really love it when we spend time together playing games or going for walks. Saying "thank you" is one way to let them know that they are important to me and make me so happy. I am very lucky!

What are you thankful for?

Tolerance

Sometimes there are things we have to put up with,
like when my baby brother won't stop crying. I know that
he's little and he can't talk yet, so it doesn't seem right for
me to be mad at him when he cries. I have to be tolerant
and patient and accept that **he isn't crying to try to
bother me.** He's just a baby.

**Was there ever a time when you had
to show tolerance?**

Trustworthiness

Have you ever made a promise? Me too! But **did you know that if you make a promise you have to keep it?** I promised my baby sister that we would play in our backyard after I finished my homework. Being honest and true to my word, I took my sister outside just like I said I would. Not only did we have a lot of fun, but my sister learned that she could trust me and that I was trustworthy.

Can you think of a time when you were trustworthy?

Values, Values, Values!

Did you know that we all have values? Some values are more important for some people than they might be for others. No matter what values you feel are important to live by, **they are your values and they belong to you!**

What are your values?

A whole Bunch of
Values

LOYOLA PRESS.
Chicago

A Whole Bunch of Values
© Copyright GEMSER PUBLICATIONS S.L., 2020
C/ Castell, 38; Teià (08329) Barcelona, Spain (World Rights)
E-mail: merce@mercedesros.com
Website: www.mercedesros.com
Tel: 93 540 13 53
Illustrator: Julia Seal
Author: Jennifer Moore-Mallinos

Published in the United States in 2022 by Loyola Press.
ISBN: 978-0-8294-5374-4
Library of Congress Control Number: 2021945745
Printed in China.